DIVIDEND GROWTH FOR RETIREMENT

DIVIDEND GROWTH FOR RETIREMENT

LUNA EMBER

CONTENTS

1 Introduction   1
2 The Importance of Dividend Growth in Retirement Pl   5
3 Building a Dividend Growth Portfolio   9
4 Strategies for Maximizing Dividend Growth   13
5 Risk Management in Dividend Growth Investing   17
6 Tax Considerations for Dividend Growth Investors   21
7 The Role of Dividend Growth in a Comprehensive Ret 23
8 Case Studies of Successful Dividend Growth Investo   25
9 Conclusion   29

Copyright © 2024 by Luna Ember
All rights reserved. No part of this book may be reproduced in any manner whatsoever without written permission except in the case of brief quotations embodied in critical articles and reviews.
First Printing, 2024

CHAPTER 1

Introduction

When it comes to retirement planning, the use of dividends, particularly reinvested dividends, as a core component for income and growth is often debated. The debate is well-warranted, especially when considering the erroneous application of reinvesting dividends without careful consideration of the purchase's sense. Reinvesting dividends paid on common stocks only makes sense if and when the purchase itself is rational. If the original terms of the deal were nonsensical, then compounding dividends is futile, particularly during the distribution phase for retirement. Dividend growth should guide which stocks you own; it should not dictate how you manage and grow your retirement fund. Tactics and strategies must align, but what works as a tactic does not always work as a strategy.

Who wouldn't want to own companies that pay out growing dividends to shareholders? The core principle is sound. Owning a portfolio of great businesses that compound their underlying per-share earnings and share more of that profit through higher cash dividend payments is fundamentally strong. Many people have made substantial wealth, slept well at night, and achieved financial freedom with this approach. The goal here is to attain a relaxed and carefree retirement with sound investments. How about you?

Purpose and Scope of the Study
Continuing the tradition of passing down a nest egg for future generations or charity, some retirees focus on income-oriented businesses. Proactive stock selection can quickly grow a portfolio, achieving a fuller measure of retirement. This study encourages retirees to seek a distinctive approach to retirement through dividend growth. This strategy does not circumvent the rigors of benchmarking chosen stocks against annuity-based compound returns in retirement planning. However, small growth of dividends is insufficient for protective investing. Stock picking within this niche lies in the moderate vicinity of short-growth assumptions and, if the stock is healthy, long-term growth over five-plus years.

Businesses bear the growing overhead of Social Security. Companies often sit on large amounts of 'tax shelter' cash, which should logically be used to increase dividend distribution and facilitate retirement trends. Paying bonuses in the form of stocks with dividends and reasonable buybacks is a corporate and social responsibility in a globally competitive environment. The dividends a company pays its shareholders should reflect a long-term strength and responsibility. Dividend growth investing is necessary for many retirees, especially when safe bond-wise investments are flat and attractive equity opportunities are dwindling.

Definition and Origins of Dividend Growth Investing
Dividend growth investing focuses on investing in companies that consistently increase their dividend payouts. This strategy relies on the return spread, where the total return comprises the dividend yield and the rate of capital appreciation. According to the value investing tradition, the principal goal of building a securities portfolio is to generate a large stream of dividends, allowing the investor to live off the dividends rather than the principal amount invested.

Investors do not need to hold onto a stock without knowing its dividend growth potential. As long as the organization is profitable and growing, future dividends are expected to increase. An increase in return is directly linked to the expectation of an increase in the dividend of an attractive company. Mutual funds focused on dividend growth stocks, with a long history of increasing dividends, are common and provide investors with a diverse basket of stocks.

CHAPTER 2

The Importance of Dividend Growth in Retirement Pl

One of the most crucial aspects of retirement planning is considering dividend growth. There are several compelling reasons why dividend growth is vital for those planning for retirement. Numerous studies have shown that dividend growth stocks have consistently been top performers among publicly traded companies over the long term. For instance, a study conducted by the University of Pennsylvania between 1926 and 2010 revealed that companies paying a steady and growing dividend provided shareholders with over 95 percent of the equity market's total return.

The Appeal of Dividend Growth

Dividend growth has become popular among many investors, both during retirement and beyond. Historically, the S&P 500 stock index has increased its dividend about two-thirds of the time, making dividend growth a significant play on the stock market. Many investment analysts argue that dividend growth over time has more reliably indicated a company's ability to weather financial turbulence. It lessens the need for investors to sell off shares during periods of market volatility. U.S. News suggests that dividend growth can position a retiree to create a portfolio "equity cushion" to meet expenses. If the value of a retiree's stock portfolio remains relatively stable over time, they can continue replacing the dividend income lost to inflation by slowly selling shares.

Historical Performance of Dividend Growth Stocks

While dividend growth may not always be the primary focus for most dividend investors, it should be. Annual dividend increases are essential for maintaining your retirement lifestyle amidst rising costs. As you plan your investment portfolio for retirement, it is crucial to build a solid foundation with high-quality dividend growth stocks. Understanding the importance of dividends and consistent dividend growth is key to benefiting your income portfolio in the long term. The longer your investment horizon until retirement, the more suitable dividend growth stocks are for both cautious and aggressive portfolios.

Historical Performance of Dividend Stocks

Over extended periods, dividend growth stocks have outperformed the market. For example, from 1910 to 2012, the S&P 500 rose an average of 9.4% annually with reinvested dividends, turning a mere $1,000 into nearly $5.25 million. However, reinvested dividends added another layer of wealth: they turned that $1,000 into an average of over $24 million (14.6% with dividends reinvested) over the same period. This reinvestment of dividends boosted the average yearly total return of the S&P 500 by nearly 5.2%. A 2003 study by Ned Davis Research Investment Climatology Group found that from 1970, 82% of the S&P 500's gains were due to reinvested dividends, with only 18% due to stock price appreciation. The S&P 500 doubled from 1998 to 2008, but without dividends, the S&P 500 price remained flat.

Dividend growth has been particularly strong during previous bear markets and recessions. For example, dividends grew considerably between 2007 and 2012. Although dividends decreased during the 2001 recession, the actual dollar dividends paid increased each year from 2001 through 2012. Dividend Growth Investing (DGI) delivers returns that generally outperform the S&P index, particularly within a 3-5 year term. Dividend growth has outperformed the S&P for 86 years. A 2011 T. Rowe Price study found that over the long term, dividend growth is the only part of the market that investors cannot participate in without holding dividend growth stocks.

CHAPTER 3

Building a Dividend Growth Portfolio

While we are concentrating in this article on a long-term perspective, it's important to note that if you're skittish about the market in the short term, or if there's uncertainty or potential loss in investments' value, you might need to reconsider stock market investments. However, maintaining a long-term horizon and consistently making purchases is a strong tenet of long-term investing. Here's a prime strategy for developing this investment plan:

1. **Selections of Dividend Growth Stocks**: Choose companies that offer direct stock purchase (DSP) programs or dividend reinvestment (DRIP) programs. Select companies that pay dividends, with at least a portion being in direct stocks or Dividend Reinvestment.
2. **Five-Year Dividend History**: Consider positions in companies that have paid dividends for at least five continuous years. Sign up for direct stock purchase or use platforms like Divotrak.

3. **Consistent Purchases**: Stay consistent with monthly purchases of one or more shares, and participate in company purchase programs or broker account transfers.
4. **Basic Research**: Perform basic research or obtain data to confirm companies with solid revenue, income growth, solid operating margins (15% or higher), low debt (not exceeding 50% of equity), and low price-to-earnings ratios (P/E ratio of less than 30).

Selecting High-Quality Dividend Growth Stocks

Finding the best dividend growth stocks may sound straightforward. You buy companies that are growing their dividends. When searching for stocks in retirement, it's important to dig deeper. We should desire stocks that can grow dividends over several years. In retirement, cash flow can sometimes be more important than stock price. Stocks with long-term growth provide protection against inflation.

Accredited investors trust stocks of companies they believe to be well-suited for long-term investment. Stocks that fit retirement investing usually serve a purpose and add value over the long term. Discussions covering these stocks will highlight additional characteristics beyond growing dividends, making the stock worth continued investment. Stocks with long-term annual dividend growth of 5% or more should be classified by sequence era.

Not all stocks with high and long-term dividend growth are of the building nature. Dividend growth stocks build value and add wealth over time through compounding. By referring to them as building nature versus trading nature, we are considering most of them for longer-term investment. Value-defining features make a stock worth investing in for retirement.

When we publish a stock in a retirement sequence, expect detailed descriptions of these characteristics. A comprehensive list of features indicating that a company is worth investing in as a retiree will be provided near the end of the current sequence. Each company in this sequence will be addressed in depth, explaining the features that make them among the best for a retirement investing plan, always capable of adding shares in retirement.

CHAPTER 4

Strategies for Maximizing Dividend Growth

In addition to investing in companies with a high probability of increasing their dividends, several other strategies can help maximize the power of dividend growth for retirement.

1. Avoid High-Yielding Stocks

Dividend growth is often more important than yield. Firms with yields exceeding 6% to 7% may struggle to grow dividends as these high yields can indicate a failure to reinvest profits adequately. One exception might be stocks acquired during a market downturn with the intention to hold them until accounting earnings rise after the recovery. At that time, dividends can be allowed to rise as a percentage of net income.

2. Choose Firms with a History of Regular and Increasing Dividends

Leveraging the principle of compound interest, earnings reported quarterly and transferred to a checking account grow more than those that remain in the same investment for several years. As of May 2013, 64 companies within the S&P 500 had increased their dividends every year for 25 years or longer, known as "dividend aristocrats." This figure may be higher, as other companies that have achieved this might be in the S&P mid-cap or small-cap benchmarks. Raising a dividend every year for at least 25 consecutive years during both good and bad times is a strong indication of a fundamentally sound firm. Small shareholders should focus on these dividend aristocrats.

3. Take Dividends in Cash During Retirement

There is ongoing debate about whether dividends should be reinvested or taken in cash for retirement expenses. Corporate finance theory suggests that dividends immediately reinvested will help funds grow faster due to compounding, ultimately resulting in a larger balance than if a cash payment had been taken. However, individual investors are taxed on the dividends they receive, so there may be no tax savings by reinvesting dividends. For funds held outside of a registered investment account, from a tax planning perspective, reinvesting dividends while in a zero or low-income tax bracket (such as during a leave of absence or early in retirement) could be advantageous.

However, reinvesting dividends adds complexity to the withdrawal process, potentially requiring the sale of a small portion of the investments each year. Therefore, the benefits of automatically reinvesting dividends for small shareholders may not be worth the effort. Including dividends as retirement income introduces enough change during retirement. Having a dividend stream already "on the books" can eliminate the need to switch from automatically reinvesting dividends to taking them in cash, freeing the investor from concerns about dividend reinvestment.

Reinvestment vs. Payout

At Dividend Power, we have illustrated extensively how the road to wealth and financial independence typically involves maximizing your dividends. By saving and living below your means, building and holding a diversified portfolio of quality dividend growth companies can create a sustainable income stream during retirement. Over time, that income can grow rapidly through the company's dividend policy, compounded by investors who reinvest those dividends back into the stocks that pay them.

To add fuel to the fire, we've examined the potential effects of the "super" model reinvestment. In this approach, a retiree invests new savings into a portfolio of the highest-yielding companies from the prior year. Reinvestment strategies are appropriate at various stages of our investing career, depending on our goals. For instance, a young accumulator with distant retirement needs will gladly reinvest dividends into the companies they rely on for growth.

The reinvestment approach is also employed by investors who have yet to retire, as a means to create a rising income stream for a time when work income will no longer be a factor. For most retirees entering or already in retirement, some form of payout approach is likely most appropriate. How and what a retiree spends will ultimately determine the best course of action regarding their dividend income. Retirees who live off dividends find company payouts crucial, with physical cash serving them best. If a retiree does not have a pressing need for the extra cash generated by their investments, they can use the collected dividends to purchase additional shares of their high-yielders.

CHAPTER 5

Risk Management in Dividend Growth Investing

When investing in businesses, it's crucial to remember that their value isn't determined minute-by-minute or day-by-day based on their stock prices. Even during the deepest depths of the pandemic, we could all probably identify at least one business that maintained an uninterrupted history of regularly increasing or stable dividend payments. In retirement, this steady march of dividend income can be relied upon, come what may. Dividend Growth Investing (DGI) isn't just about seeking higher yields. Many of us aren't overly concerned with yield unless we're still in the accumulation phase and reinvesting. Otherwise, the increasing yield-on-cost in the portfolio is likely to "keep up" with and eventually surpass inflation.

It makes little sense to consider selling shares of the underlying businesses unless they deteriorate and no longer meet our entry or quality criteria. The worst investor experience of holding the entire S&P 500 index occurred for those who sold at the low point in early 2009. In my opinion (and others'), that kind of panic-selling risk largely disappears if one is well-diversified into 35, 45, 55, or 65 positions rather than a carefully selected handful. For the retired dividend growth investor with a limited window of time in a 30-year retirement, a superior business bought at the best possible price may hopefully provide a stable and increasing income stream (dividends) even if the total return, including the capital value of stocks held, takes a hit.

Diversification Strategies

In risk management, diversification is a crucial principle. There are many types of diversification methods, including asset, time, and place diversification. We will focus on asset allocation when it comes to diversification, as geographic distribution requires a lot of expertise in different parts of the world. Market timing is generally not feasible according to the body of evidence. Diversification has the ability to reduce risk and decrease losses compared to single-stock or small-stock holdings.

For example, holding 10 stock donors may not provide you with cash, while a $5 Omni annual lender will. Another way to reduce risk is to increase trade size to lower interest rates when expanding your franchise. Investing in these additional opportunities can be a smarter approach for retirees looking to diversify their positions fully.

Additionally, diversification grows the risk-reward ratio. By holding more than 30 deposits, one reduces a lot of personal investments and their investment portfolios. This reduces the impact that news about a particular stock can have on your portfolio. Over time, the ups and downs of the many stocks in your portfolio should even out. An investor can also evaluate more business models and each fund's investment strategies, such as corporate policies, ability to increase market share, and the provision of products and services in constant demand. These businesses should maintain a modest level of debt, varying from 0% to 40% of equity, and a high income and ROI.

For companies with barriers to entry protecting their proprietary power, high growth may not necessarily equate to dividend revenue streams, but these companies seem to have comprehensive long-term financial planning. Retirees can benefit from these strategies.

CHAPTER 6

Tax Considerations for Dividend Growth Investors

If you're considering dividend growth as a way to fund your retirement years, it's essential to think about tax considerations. Often overlooked in decision-making regarding dividend growth investing is the maxim of Wall Street: try to align your investments with appropriate accounts given strategies and sector concentration. If this thought has never crossed your mind, it's time to consider tax implications as you embark on retirement investing. The goal of this series on adapting dividend growth for retirement plans is to spotlight investments that are at least tax-efficient, if not outright tax-advantaged.

First, the great news about investing in dividend growth is that the tax implications can largely be minimized. Since money for long-term stocks should be kept in taxable accounts that you won't draw funds from frequently, we only need to concern ourselves with the inevitable: dividends and capital gains for those stocks that are briefly held will be taxed at favorable long-term rates. But for the most part, my fellow dividend growth investors and I can just watch that compounding safely grow, especially when reinvesting in the first half of our careers and leaving cash dividends in our portfolio for withdrawal beyond 60. One significant tax-related decision we might make is during a major final portfolio reshaping, where you get to reposition large amounts at low prices. This is in direct contrast to ongoing dividend growth investing.

Tax-Efficient Investing Strategies

As a dividend growth investor, several tax-efficient investing strategies are worth considering. While tax issues imply individual strategies, some general principles apply. You'll generally want to invest in tax-advantaged accounts if the funds in those accounts are intended for your retirement. Investing in dividend growth stocks is typically beneficial, but minimizing your tax liabilities is equally important. This means learning which types of dividends are more or less tax-efficient.

Tax considerations might also lead you to alternative strategies, such as investing in low-turnover and traditional growth stocks. It might encourage you to focus on your asset allocation or the placement of assets in appropriate shelters or accounts. The most tax-efficient strategy for you will depend on several factors, including how much you have in different sheltered or non-sheltered stock accounts, how long until retirement, your overall asset allocation, other savings, and, of course, current or anticipated tax policy.

A significant part of most dividend growth investing strategies involves the careful acquisition of a slowly constructed portfolio over a considerable period. This includes adding a few shares to existing positions or exchanging relatively small amounts of stock. In his 2015 analysis of the impact of taxes on individual investors' portfolios, J.P. Morgan's Michael Liersch reflects that an investor's time horizon is a critical factor in reducing taxes as a portion of their overall return.

CHAPTER 7

The Role of Dividend Growth in a Comprehensive Ret

In a nutshell, the income produced by regularly increasing dividends provides retirees with a raise every year, keeping pace with inflation. Regularly increasing dividends offer built-in protection against inflation, which can erode the purchasing power of a stagnant income. Over time, the boost from growing dividends helps offset rising living expenses.

Dividend growth aligns with retirees' ongoing need to supplement other retirement income sources—such as Social Security, pensions, or other annuities—with reliable, potentially growing income. While a current yield meets retirees' immediate income needs, a growing income enhances income streams for later years. Growing income from dividends can hedge against the end of employment income by improving a portfolio's sustainable withdrawal rate. Research suggests that portfolios with reliable dividend income can support higher withdrawal rates and that a dividend-growth strategy provides a higher probability of never running out of money compared to relying solely on aggressive growth or a fixed approach.

Integration with Other Retirement Income Sources

Many financial advisors recognize the role that dividend growth can play in meeting retirees' income needs. In this section, we explore how dividend growth integrates with other sources of guaranteed income. Understanding how dividend growth ties into Social Security, pensions, and even the growth of home equity will provide a unique perspective on a retiree's portfolio.

Coordination of Income Sources: When planning for retirement, income sources must be forecasted and coordinated to ensure they are distributed throughout retirement. This involves deciding which sources to draw from first, when to activate other income sources, and understanding the tax implications. Dividend payments might affect taxes, possibly as rates for qualified dividends or rising rates for long-term capital gains.

Dividends are often coordinated with the sale of a home later in retirement. If needed, the home can be refinanced as part of the liquidity strategy, providing cash that isn't interest rate dependent and is available for spending. When the house is eventually sold—to live with family, move to a retirement facility, or leave a legacy—the housing function can be modified to provide liquidity.

CHAPTER 8

Case Studies of Successful Dividend Growth Investo

Below are the stories of several real-life dividend growth investors. Their stories are valuable as they explain what these individuals did and why. Just as important is how they did it, which is clearly shown in the statistics, though using end-of-year 2004 data. We know their investment strategies worked well beyond 2005-2006, as sound strategies remain effective over time. What follows are excerpts from these investors' interviews, including insights into their approaches and interests.

Greg Dinger: Dividend Growth for Retirement

Greg Dinger has used dividends multigenerationally as an indicator of good, buy-and-hold companies. The first principle he followed is: it's better to have dividends in hand than to hope for gains from selling shares. He believes dividend growth investing is a solid retirement plan because purchasing dividend-paying stocks lowers the volatility of his overall portfolio. Reinvesting both the automatic savings program and the dividends boosts the accumulation speed of appreciating assets. It also forces the investor to ignore negative news and events that occur during investing. Lowered volatility and sticking to your plan are essential in retirement savings.

Focused on retirement investing, Greg moved to individual stocks as soon as the index/mutual funds in his accounts had enough value to sell without penalties. He switched to individual dividend growth stocks about 8-9 years ago after cashing out of JDPower, one of the early Rob Dingman DFA portfolios. His IRAs with Morningstar Div 10 or with TSM or SCV can self-direct into individual dividend growth stocks at Vanguard, allowing him to move funds without penalty. He started following and investing in most of the DGdModel suggested stocks about 6-7 years ago.

Key Takeaways and Lessons Learned

Elizabeth, a retired financial advisor, began investing her inheritance in dividend-paying stocks that offered dividend growth. She sought growing income that would outpace inflation. Elaine, who retired from magazine publishing at age 55 in 2003, focused on dividends for living expenses. She appreciated that her dividends increased almost every quarter, helping her manage inflation.

Sandi, an investor from Minnesota now in her early 70s, has always liked dividend-paying stocks. Her interest grew in the late 1970s after meeting Geraldine Weiss, the first woman to become a financial analyst and a top stock picker. One of Sandi's investments is in a well-known company: "Everybody knows Rohm & Haas paint," Sandi said. "I've had Rohm & Haas for a long time. I also started investing in Webster Financial because I think dividends will become a much better deal."

From these case studies, eight key takeaways and lessons have emerged:

1. **Dividends provide a better retirement income stream.**
2. **Dividends give you real money to spend, save, invest, or give away as you choose.**
3. **Dividend growth protects you from inflation.**

4. **Companies that increase their dividends tend to see share prices rise, too.** Investment guru Jeremy Siegel suggests buying dividend-paying stocks when their yields are rising or high "in relation to both their own history and the yield on AAA-rated corporate bonds."

CHAPTER 9

Conclusion

In this work, we develop the notion of using dividend growth as a method to secure a retirement income in a more straightforward manner than many approaches available today. The Monte Carlo results are particularly illuminating, suggesting that the likelihood of failure is small and that using historical average values for parameters significantly increases the probability of success. Somewhat counterintuitively, simplicity in approach works for retirement-income investors.

Further research can now follow, including ways to smooth the likely path for dividend income and evaluate alternatives to dividends as the source of retirement income, such as net withdrawals including capital sales as in the Perpetual Withdrawal Plan and Sequence Risk literature. Alternatively, one could test eliminating steps from the simple method described above, such as removing the buffer portfolio, to see what effect this has on the outcome. The simple general rule described by Guyton does not seem to improve the withdrawal path, and neither does it seem to alleviate the early retiree's difficult 'death spiral' problem described by Kitces. A successful retirement income for life needs either a very large trend of increasing withdrawals with few or no subsequent decreases, or protective steps and costs as described in the overall open sequence of return, or OSOR, literature complete with the 'unintuitive result' of flexible rather than fixed withdrawals. Retirees simply reducing their equity will likely find their continuously declining dividend incomes and continued devaluation of their secure dividend increases to be unlikely paths to riches.

Summary of Findings

Throughout this essay, I have outlined numerous benefits of living off dividends during retirement. The core idea here is that dividend growth is better suited for the retiree with a long-term view. The goal is to set oneself up to maintain a relative level of income for longer than expected, easing the potential anxieties retirees often bear. My initial assumption was that those relying on dividend growth over other retirement options, such as the 4% rule, are bearing more risk than necessary in the long run. However, as we explore different aspects of dividend growth, we find this isn't exactly the case. Although I do not agree with some of the exaggerated claims offered in favor of this method, dividend growth certainly has merits when considering retirement income.

I argue that living off dividend growth alone means accepting three things: firstly, it limits the investor to relatively conservative investment options; secondly, the investor is actually selling off shares of their principal, albeit small fractional shares; and thirdly, there is risk that arises based on the first two points. In reviewing how dividends are taxed in conjunction with these points, one will find that this strategy can work. The individual must limit themselves to a decent-to-stretched level of income to keep this strategy sustainable. While most will find the potential benefits of investing in stocks to be outweighed by the risk, this is not the main goal. We cannot ignore the risks—there are opportunities within, sure—but risks nonetheless. At the foundation, though, we know that most retirees will find great comfort and appreciation in not running out of money during their later years.

Future Research Directions

Based on the existing literature and the findings of this study, there appears to be a lack of research focusing on how the importance of dividend growth for retirement planning is influenced by the number of years until retirement. This should be the next focus of research in the well-explored area of the relative importance of dividends and growth for stock prices concerning retirement planning. Future research could focus on alternative methodologies and solutions for determining the essential features of stock value that firms can influence while remaining consistent with the poorly-diversified investor's economic dependence on retirement.

Additionally, pioneering studies on the importance of dividend policy for home-cooked investments should aim at two additional criteria in their solutions: (1) the solution must reveal what stock valuation factors are within the firm's control and can inform the manager's choice of dividend policy; and (2) the solution must result in a dividend policy consistent with the requirement that the firm finance all investments, retire all debt, and pay all dividends strictly from its current and projected operating cash flows. No studies have met these two additional criteria. While it may be challenging to satisfy these criteria, the back-slave criteria upon which they were chosen may be easily abandoned. Determining the merit of this suggestion would be an important contribution to the literature. Finally, as Arnold and De Mello have indicated, future research might draw a continuum of deduction as the size of the retired investor's stock portfolio becomes larger, thus reducing the necessity for such research on the effect.

Milton Keynes UK
Ingram Content Group UK Ltd.
UKHW031352011224
451755UK00004B/366